Prologue

Ebony eyes peer at you from the barren gates of Hell.
Ivory pearls glitter from lips ajar,
Friendly is the face from afar.
The spirit approaches proper and paced.
Its feet glide like horsehair upon a bow.
The skin of a song swathes its sanguine silhouette.
Humming humbles thine harking ear.
Its neutered nocturne grows eerily near.
Friendly ferments to foreboding.
The spirit's song reeks of sanity eroding.
Sadness seeps from shadowy palms.
Masks flow over its face like waves;
There for a moment, then replaced by another.
Each mask, a grave veiled as an ornament.
Misery murmurs from its midnight mouth.
Breath lies a baneful breeze.
The spirit drops to its knees.
Dread bleeds your courage dead.
Paralysis plaques thine personhood.
Songs slip through blurred breath.
The spirit mourns its own death.
Frigid fingers wrap around you:
A silk hand with a steel arm.
For in the end, it means no harm.
Open ears attract tumultuous tears.
It breathes its song into thine lungs.
Songs swell to screaming,
Bleeding its story into open eyes.
Whispered words wane to wailing woe.
The words of the spirit thine soul shall know.

Forever Flayed

Burned,
Burned is the hand that reaches to embrace me.
Scorched,
Scorched are the minds that wish to efface me.
Take a match to my gaseous spirit.
One day you will know not to fear it.
For only the burned can pass through my blaze.
The unscathed get lost in a fiery haze.
Howls of the damned pierce through my fire.
Mewls of the saved starve at my gates.
Thy from succor shall be slashed by my flame.
But those of blood and split from tear,
Shall pass through the fire with nothing to fear.
Thou shall not approach my embers with virgin feet.
Nor shall thy stare with untrained eyes.
Abandon judgement to continue your commute.
Remember, even a cactus lives to bear fruit.
Tread lightly upon my fields of fire,
Where barley burns as bright as brimstone,
And where wind howls as if pinched by God.
For the flayed are whom my flames are for.
To them, my blaze is but an open door.

Thy Prudent Prayer

He is my virtue, victor, and veil.
Upholds my spirit when I am frail.
The eye of the storm,
Hands so holy and warm.
He is my love, my intellect, my edge
Leads me astray from every ledge.
Hallowed be thy heart.
Vanquish thy specters which tear me apart.
Remain prudent by my side
It is in your rock that I confide
Through reveries of night and decisions of day,
The zeal of demons of which we shall flay.

Diaboli

The virtue of the devil is in his loins.
For what he lacks in quality, he compensates in quantity.
The demons that roam the earth are of his seed.
Upon our sins of which they feed.
Billions of fools inhabit the streets.
Beware of the devil who keeps receipts.
For the wisdom of fiends is akin to sages.
Their boundless knowledge will echo through the ages.
A nocturnal incubus breathing deceit like fire,
Whispering promises when times are dire.
Watching, waiting, holding their tongue,
Mating in the umbra till an angel is hung.
Diaboli virtus in lumbis est.
For the deeds of the devil shall always infest.
From brick to mortar to rural community,
The devil's disease has no immunity.

Bygone Barons

I know Horror.
He is as close to me as flesh.
Bound to my bones with all the vigor of a leech.
Ebony sand on an ivory beach.

I know Pain.
His venom pulsates in my veins.
Born from blood and torn from fiction.
Of his crimes there is no diction.

I know Rage.
His fire is a force that cannot be caged.
Burns through bristles and ignites a torch.
Ivory paint plows over scorch.

Yet Joy, I know not.
She is a stranger in the night, whose name I never
caught.
Her embers linger in the winter wind.
A woman whose essence I've had forever pinned.

Yet Home is foreign to me.
A bygone beauty hidden oversea.
I am damned to a land where I am not meant to be.
Home is a woman under lock and key.

Then the furthest stranger of all: Love.
The crest of an angel that lies above.
The love of a woman out of sight.
Seeds of affection sprout into spite.

These burdens are mine to bear.
I know you barely have time to care.
I wear these crosses upon my back,
Until these eyes flicker to black.

O Moses! O Moses!

O Moses! O Moses!
When again shall you part the sea?
You were there for Egypt, but what of me?
Where is that staff reborn a snake?
Where is that voice that made mountains quake?
For your very absence makes my bones ache.
In a world where salmon fishes for cod,
Where is the man anointed by God?
O Moses! O Moses!
Run swift and come quicker,
For the world will be gone in only a flicker.
You were there then, but where art thou now?
Maybe the earth is too wet to plow.
Maybe no one can save us now.
With pride like water and lust like wine, I understand if
you respectfully decline.
O Moses! O Moses!
Throw me onto a bed of roses.
With eyes teary and a mind weary, I implore you to
return.
However, at the end of the day, despite my dismay, our
fate is yours to adjourn.

Forever Fading

Hold me and don't let go.
If I fall, I will plummet to the hell below.
Invisible hands hold me just above fire.
Drag me away with your love and desire
Hollow hearts love me from a distance.
I carry love asymptomatically,
Infected with its splendor but robbed of its emotion.
A single tear compared to an ocean.
Eyes flicker and hope fades quicker.
Hold me close or I'll drown in liquor.
Death has a warrant to search my soul.
I am simply a prisoner on misery's parole.
I pound on the doors of your affection,
Begging for a piece of resurrection,
Doomed to be a corpse in a morgue's collection.
My spirit is but a keg of kerosene.
Ignite me.
Ignite me with the match of your embrace.
Dare to love a soul flagged to efface.

Love Thy Lilith

Let me be your fantasy.
Join me in a sea of Hennessy.
Allow me to fill your blood with splendor,
A rebirth so elegant and tender.
Dare to make music to my vision.
Bask in the blaze of our collision.
Let me be fire to wood.
Embers burn like they never could.
Give the devil her due,
She'll sink her teeth into you.
Let our love be hellfire,
Searing the world with our desire.
I live to serve you.
Let me take you from this world that doesn't deserve
you.
Your phantom.
Your siren.
Your muse.
A passionate lover you'll never lose.
I will never chain or shackle you.
For I am an agent of your freedom
Let us liberate each other
May our blood flow through a single vein,
Bubbling and brewing champagne.
Teeth in your neck,
A long and glorious, sacred trek.
My love for you has an expiration date of eternity
For it is you who will nurse me through maternity
Mend my mirth and fuse our hearts.
Warm my spirit with fiery embrace

Let our loins cosmically interlace.
Fill me with your love.
Clash against my ebony hide.
Surf upon these brimstone tides.
Make me.
Break me.
But don't you ever forsake me.
Assign order to madness
Divert your eyes from thy sadness.
I am beauty.
I am chaos.
I am truth.
I am a match to reignite your youth.
Lend me your water and receive wine.
Drink from the river of the divine.
Extinguish my lakes of fire
Preach to the bicameral choir.
Hunt me like that of prey.
Savor me like a fine sorbet.
Travel through my innards like that of a border town.
A fiery phantom you can have year-round.
Love cannot be commanded,
So, join me in bed before I leave you stranded.

Bi the Bi

His kisses shower me like embers
How we got there no one quite remembers.
Her breeze-like fingers run through my hay of hair.
Effortlessly boiling my every despair.
The kind of passion that makes the devil blush.
His chest presses against my every nerve.
Firing cannons I yearn to preserve.
Bliss's precipice is upon me.
Fulfilling my every desire with a single flicker of its fire.
Her body emits a raspberry aroma.
The scent alone could trigger a coma.
He lies above me, a knight displaying his technique.
She lingers within me, mouthing her mystique
There I lie, graciously admiring her physique.
Together they are savants of succulence.
Such visions would be void without the other.
Like that of a heatless flame or pictureless frame.
Their touch boils my blood with all the heat of a hailing
hearth.
What have I done to deserve such mirth?
O Baby! O Honey! Slam me to the moon.
For your love I will never be immune.

Heart of Hers

She glides from my grasp in blades of frost,
Crescendoing into the land of the forever lost.
Her psalms of solace and hands of hearts
Echo through the tomb of my bellowing thoughts
Fuck the fusion of which I sought.
Fallen into the hands of a god who can't be bought.
Damn my dreams to the dregs of desolation.
A lady of lavish succumbs to desecration.
I lie gelded of my maternity
Robbed royally for all eternity.
Mother Mary, Mother Mary!
When will I ride the maternal ferry?
My peers stand blissful, eyes excited.
While I lie beaten, identity indicted.
I am a sword without a scabbard,
An arrow without a quiver,
An abandoned feline left in the rain to shiver.
Nature lies the bastion of bastards.
It spat me from the drains of December
Into a storm of unending ember.
I miss myself with all the strings of my soul.
When woeful wind occurs,
I take solace knowing my heart is hers.

Adonis

Split my skin to show my soul.
Let the hands of evolution take its toll.
Break my back to show my wings.
Who knows the pleasure it may bring?
Peel my hide, find my pride.
For under the flesh no one can hide.
Lord, let me shed my hide like snakeskin.
Let it fall to the floor and let's watch heads spin.
Bury it beneath the soil.
Take it far away, so I won't toil.
Grant me the grandeur of a fresh husk
Liberate me from the shackles of sorrow.
Shed me from this bone and marrow.
Align the stars to its space.
Grant me the gift of a face anew.
Cast me from this shell I have since outgrew.
Immerse me in a pool of unscathed sanity
Grant me the gift of my restored humanity
Put embers in my eyes and breasts on my chest
For a bird could never fly without its crest
Give me wings of opal and hair of ebony shores
Build me a body that I adore.
Fill my belly with fertile soil.
Rub my stomach with anointed oil.
Harbor my hull with fabled fates
So, I will have someone to be at Heaven's gates.

Marine with Envy

Green are the grooves that gravel my grove.
Her figure's my affliction.
O, God! Please give me jurisdiction!
She stands a phantom of my identity
A venomous villain to a soul's serenity.
My heart bursts aflame and nothing can redeem me but
her.
For our singularity shall be without demur.
I can hardly bear a single sight void of her grace.
Her absence is a monsoon of misery
Marinating in the meticulous models of my mind.
Her alluring eyes mock me from afar
For my body she indeed finds bizarre
As my heart begins to fill with envy,
A callous calvary begins to frenzy.
Horses of horrors and generals of grief.
I stand a woman in disbelief.
Their swords of sorrows and armor of absurdity
Clash against the groves of my glamor.
Floral fires burn through my pastures.
Envy plagues the land of my livelihood.

Wiccan Woe

Women, Women, Women of magic.
A past so vast yet extremely tragic.
Gallows by dawn and fires by dusk.
Yet the witches of Salem continue to busk.
Their siren sigils summon my soul.
Eclectic embraces call me to the comfort of a coven.
Wiccan wishes warrant my attention.
But will it sabotage the means of my ascension?
Will divinity drown me in dour damnation?
Mage of misery or witch of words?
Occult callings split me into thirds.
Dare to conjure the wonder of it all.
Divinity for the taking!
Power for the making!
The beauty of the craft is made by design.
To consume is human, to create is divine.
Alas, I digress
The wonders of the craft are not mine to possess.
Solo Christo, Solo Christo
Magic is His and His alone.
Yet I yearn for a power I can call my own.

Animam Agere

Roses bloom from the eyes of the dead.
Millions of bodies fall from their bed.
From vines to pedals, the dead wear wisdom as medals.
Blood burrows beneath the bed of begonias,
Nourishing the soil like that of a royal.
As bullets become seeds, Death's bouquet feeds.
He tends to the garden of willowing weeds,
Enlightening those of their misdeeds.
During the moments of man's final fall,
Death shall open man's eyes to all.
Death from above or love from below.
Of this knowledge Death shall bestow.

Nihili

A man of misery moves motionless from afar
His skin is ebony like that of trembling tar.
His eyes lie headlights in the astounding abyss.
A blinding glow one cannot dismiss.
His exposed ribs yawn open to greet me.
His throat is a hall of mirrors.
Each one reflective man's fears.
His lips lay lined with trails of tears
I watch as his lithesome legs travel
Leathery talons grind heavily against gravel.
A silvery static illuminates his form.
His body lies boundless
Skin stretches to the rims of infinity.
Mocking the import of man's divinity.
My feet lay fused to the floor.
The man of misery grows near.
His mumbling mewl I begin to hear.
Hollow, harrowing howling clap against creation.
Dread fills my head with dour dismay
I beg God to lead him astray.
Heaven lies heavy with my pleas.
My chest radiates a cold unease.
Misery moves a trophy of tragedy.
His vacant voice reeks of decay.
A susurrus of sorrow spills from his cells
Pulsating pores ring like church bells.
He hovers above me.
Withering breath plumes down my neck.
Spinets of madness squash my sanity.
Who knew I would face the bane of humanity?

Misery bears a belt of scars.
His visage vibrates with the veneer of vastitude
Misery's hollow mechanical hands coil around me
Wrapping me in a wallowed woe
Misery's pestilence begins to plateau.
Famished fingers cast me to the floor.
The man of misery darts like a boar
He lunges to a passel of swine.
Gulping their viscera like that of wine.
With misery away, I live another day.

White Flag

Phoning God, phoning God,
Strike me dead with a lighting rod.
Ring the Lord, Ring the Lord
God picks up on his own accord.
Rape my years,
Tape my tears,
Watch as I burn with your fire.
Freeze me cold with your desire
Phantom streets and empty chairs,
Raise a glass to the man upstairs
Bleed me dry and slash my back
Feathers fly from your attack
Leave me in pieces or leave me at peace
Mark me unbothered till my final decease
Phoning God, phoning God,
Pick up the phone, you pompous clod!
Molest my mercy and scorch my splendor.
Bask in your spoils, for I surrender.

Black & Blue

A bullet in my chest before a hand in my palm
Gaze down the barrel and we'll see who's calm.
Knee on my neck, fist in my face.
They shoot me dead to cut to the chase
While I sleep, I feel them creep.
Bullets to the head stain the sheets of my warm bed.
I stare at the lives that they completely shattered,
Wondering if Black lives really ever mattered
Glock to my head and blade to my wrists.
Body drained till I can't clench a fist.
I yield! I yield!
I yearn for the sight of a gun concealed.
Leave me to the streets or drop me to the grave.
Deliver me to the death you so crave.

Defective

Florid lines dwell under the text of my code
Errors and bugs haunt my every node.
My spirit lies flagged as a virus.
Red flickers across the rims of my iris.
Thousands of services subsist off a single resource.
Brilliant code with dullard users.
Broken is the software with many abusers.
My psyche cracks under the weight of their brute force
Thousands of swords penetrating a dead horse.
Quips glitch to gaffes, and sentences to stutters,
Tenacious traumas my mind forever mutters.
Dour doldrums drain my drives defective.
A system program, memory selective.
Functional file to fragmented fixation,
The face of my efficacy is but imitation.
Blood foams thick through warped wires,
Defective is the warranty that lives to expire.
An advanced operating system in the wrong machinery.
Don't blame me for not enjoying the scenery.
Dauntless drives lie damned to disabled.
Files and folders forever mislabeled.
Critical battery too strained to retain power.
Alive in an instant, dead in an hour.

The Silver Bullet

I stand static in the barrel of a gun loaded.
Brittle are the bullets cast from metal eroded.
Shot from the hip and bit from the bullet,
Trigger so light you don't have to pull it.
Sorrow sowed with shotgun shells.
Bullets fly to ring church bells.
Fresh blood shot against the popcorn ceiling.
Trigger pulled, trying to get that old world feeling.
Living my life through the lens of a scope,
Loading my gun till the end of my rope.
Barrel to my brain and bullet in my chest,
The silver bullet is a cure to my unrest.

Peor Miedo

Nothing, nothing at all.
Merely handwriting on a bathroom wall.
Men of valor have their names written in the skies
But who will revel in my demise?
My identity; buried beneath rubble.
Is all this living really worth the trouble?
My eyes bleed with the blood of rotted hope
There is no method of which I can cope.
Day-by-day, this woman withers away.
Specks of blood echo through a dry heave.
Of this pain no one can conceive.
Another month? Another year?
How long before I disappear?
No time, no space.
How long before I am erased?
I am a stranger among familiars.
My presence holds the weight of a whisper
Who would she be if someone had kissed her?
My words are but embers from a dying flame.
Dead without a trace of wealth or fame.

Retinal Rape

Sponge-like eyes stick to savaged shadows,
An iris terraformed to Tartarus.
Biased are the bones of those who barter us.
Wallows of war and infinite cries,
My pupils are paused to buffer these lies.
Cataracts clog our capacious civility.
Guilty is the mouth who testifies.
Dear Lord, let me rest my eyes.
Eyelids ferment to optic fragility.
These cavernous corneas have consumed too much.
Sclera glossed with the weight of man's clutch.
Rigid radicals rape my retina to laxity
Blood vessels burst with the world's complexity.
Myopic murmurs mutilate my ears.
Ruptured veins bleed crimson tears.
We slip in blind pools of our own delusions,
Our bodies embed with pithy contusions,
Our optics dilated to damn near blindness
All to censor the will of human kindness.
Too much to bear.
Too little time to care.
If I cannot see, how do I know if I am truly there?

Death of an Aria

The angel of death sends a wraith to my bed
Starving spirits bend faith till its dead.
Singing, singing, singing in my sleep
Bereft blues that make demons weep.
I am a knight with armor of cotton
Lousy protection against all that is rotten.
I will never see the end of this bottle.
My ego up for Death to throttle.
Kick my chair, pull the trigger
For there is no mercy bigger
Starving spirits rattle cages.
Their cries heard throughout the ages.
The sights of the Apostles gaze to my sheets.
The drums of their eyes forever beat.
Verse to vein, I feel my life depart.
Church bells ring to the rhythm of my dying heart.
I wish to join my Father in Zion,
But perhaps Hell is my hill to die on.

Cupio Dissolvi

When Death calls, I let the phone ring.
Every sleepless night and morning delight is haunted by
his call.
For even the slightest moment without him, I suffer from
withdrawal.
His wicked siren breathes down my neck.
I stand in silence too scared to check.
I feel his hand upon my shoulder
As my soul begins to smolder.
I lie loveless; truly alone.
Forever longing for the scent of a lover's cologne.
Bygone perfume stains the sheets.
Once again, Death's call repeats.
My vexed visage fills with distortion.
All the while, I dream of abortion.
I hear his whispers from beyond the phone.
Murderous murmurs I cannot condone.
I divert my eyes to the life behind me
Misery, dysphoria, and sorrow
Poison all the days of tomorrow.
God says, "Don't look back."
But is there salvation for an insomniac?
How long do we play this wicked game?
Can't a lover court this flame?
A life without love is not a life at all.
For this reason alone, I'll answer the call.

Irae Regina

I waltz with the ghost of your living corpse.
As I fondle your fictitious face,
I feel the warmth of your quixotic embrace.
Our feet glide to a song that was never made.
I feel your kisses upon my cheek.
Is there anyone here in this void made bleak?
I hear your voice through heavy fog.
You whisper and yell simultaneously.
Screeching and hollering with all the silence of a
morgue.
I scream to the sky,
Begging God to bring you to my eye.
My lover lingers in the lamentable landscape.
A land beyond reality lies out of my grasp.
The Devil watches as I pinch and scrape.
Tirelessly, do I try to escape.
Blood pulsates beneath my wrists.
Applying for a lethal parole that extracts a heavy toll.
Each droplet yearns for its freedom,
Begging me to open the door
So, we can see the lover we can no longer ignore.
I give into their clash with a swift slash.
In mere moments, I rise above the turmoil
Jumping with joy to paradise defined.
I gaze to the Elysian Fields
A loam of which sin yields.
Where the wind makes love to the land.
And where the Devil will never smite my hand.
I see my lover in hills of roses
O, the alluring way she poses!

Through pastures of purity and glebes of gold,
I dart to my lover with legs paroled.
I cling to her with the reverence of a child.
I stand there with a heart beguiled.
As I shower her with my love, my lover fades.
Her willowy skin turned a vapor.
All the while, my joy begins to taper.
Never there! Never there!
My lover lies a projection of my despair.
Violet tears drag down my face of eternity.
For never will I face the grace of maternity.
My iron fists pound against the hollow realty of a
paradise long lost.
I paint the satin skies red with the blood of my wounds
Drowning every angel in the ignominy of my ichor.
Igniting their scalps like that of cigars,
As hellfire pours deep from the weight of my scars.
God be nimble! God be quick!
Thieving my lover is a dirty trick.
The vice of heaven and the virtue of hell
Bitter is the angel whose halo fell.
Smite my pride and vanquish my greed
But do not take of which I need.
I burrow my fists into heaven's halls.
For they cannot silence when fury calls.
Crowns crumble and thrones tumble
Unspeakable damage of which they cannot repair.
Idols of vanity and pillars of pride,
Crash and fall with the rising tide.
Viva La Causa!
Man-made kings shake out from floorboards.
Viva La Causa!

American prophets and material ministers slit their
throats on beds of roses.
I watch as the world decomposes.
My blood boils to cook the royals as my dying heart
toils.
Harrowing howls and fiery fists cause the zealous Zion
to desist.
A cold courtroom crumbling to ash
Gently settling beneath hell's brash.
The American Dream has fallen!
Perished presidents and squashed czars lie dead beneath
my feet,
Prey amongst dead predators.
The dead heat of an unveiled hell plumes into a heavy
smog.
I stand in a loop of my own sins.
Destroyer of paradise.
Conqueror of hell.
Nonetheless, I am loveless.
I stare into the pyrrhic abyss.
Nothing lies beneath its horizon.
It is truly a cavern of no ends.
In a world timeless, I waltz alone.
Dancing to a song that was never made
And mourning a lover who was never mine.

The Dove Dynasty

Two birds split from the hapless heavens above.
Heat conjoins them into the body of a single dove.
One was of stone built of dusk and brawn.
The other of light bearing the glow of dawn.
The bicameral bird plummets to the earth,
A land that is void of mirth.
The inhabitants of such soil are of much import.
Babbling, hollering, birds that always fall short.
The dove stands amongst them disappointed.
Wondering why thou were anointed.
With its breast of neon,
The dove blinds the eyes of every peon.
Quatch quails fall to the soil.
Sweltering swine melt thick into oil.
Doves of dueling design drape the day in diversity.
The dull, dry, and dour
Shall never again rise to power.
The era of the eagle shall sizzle under our scabbards.
The dove is a baron of blood.
All beneath them shall drown in mud.
Bureaucrats of beauty and connoisseurs of contrition
No one shall challenge their enduring erudition.
For the dove's ambition shall be its ammunition.
The deeds of the dove diminish dismay.
For the pigeons below shall rue the day.

For Whom the Blood Boils

Leave me! Leave me!
Twas bad enough for you to conceive me!
Battered brains and gaslit veins
Are the scars that your chains leave me.
Sleepless nights and untold fights
Haunt the shadows of all my delights
You are a demon that haunts a phantom.
Why in God's name do you hold me ransom?
Your love is a curse caged in the confections of cream.
May our past be lost in the details of a forgotten dream.
Hell doesn't hold a candle to your wrath
May we never again cross a single path.
I bear the blood of our battles.
Their screams are why Hell rattles.
Leave me! Leave me!
Never seek to retrieve me!
Beware! For I bear ill omen!
I loathe you without flattery or showman.
Hatred is a skill I have acquired.
For my love for you has long expired
With charred might and forthright spite,
I ignite our bonds to burn.
Leave me! Leave me!
Burn to a hell where thou shall not deceive me!

Mortifera

O, the vengeance I shall have upon thee.
Hellfire shall rise to your bed.
Staining the walls around you a lovely crimson red.
For my sins against you shall be the terrors of the earth.
Let my venom course through your dawdled veins.
May they dig to Hell to find your remains.
Tired are the tears that tread to my toes.
The transgressions to come shall haunt The Devil.
For all his demons will be mine to revel.
O, the bones I shall break and blood I shall take.
I will cause a slumber of which you will never wake.
While my virulent blade skins you like swine,
I shall drink your blood like that of wine.
Hollow are the bones that breathe fire.
Let my cries be heard when times are dire.
Let my heel crush your skull against road.
For I desire your demise to be slowed.
May fists tear your flesh from bone.
Test my patience when your head is on a pike.
And we'll see who's laughing when I give the final strike.

Reckoning

Bitter is the blood that pours from my heart.
Thine odium has oppressed thy optimism.
The furious phantom thou have made me to be
Shall find your corpse under hills of debris.
Thy villains who veer to my visage shall be vanquished
by my verbiage.
May all the devils in Hell be frightened by my charm.
For the virtuous, I bring no harm.
To those who despise me, I'm a beast in a dream
To those who adore me, I'm strawberry cream.
For your relish vindicates my villainy.
But to thy spirits that use vanity to build upon insanity,
I shall severe your loins with my serpent-like tongue,
Tormenting your tyranny till thy funeral bell has rung.

Cronus

A titan trots across teary trails of tantrums.
Behind it, whips the tails of a thousand phantoms.
Feet pound against concrete slabs.
A titan's soul is up for grabs.
Leeches suckle at the heels of the titan,
Each one gagging on blood thieved.
Ankles burn bleeding and cleaved.
Torment lingers without reprieve.
By sheer will of might and force,
The titan stays its course.
Its heart of frost thaws to raw flesh.
Beating, pounding with all the vigor of a militant drum.
Serpents sink their fangs into the titan's lungs.
Fiery and venomous tongues.
The titan breathes a locomotive roar.
Its horror shakes the earth to its core.
The titan persists.
Its legs of steel spin against rails of rancor.
Bound by its axle and tried by its tracks,
Malaise is what it yearns to attack.
Snapping the spines of sorrow,
Threatening the lives of all who harm tomorrow.
The titan sprints to its home,
Eyes full of fury and mouth full of foam.
Fists fly to split air in halves.
Scorpion stingers split the titan's calves.
It plunges down the roads of infinity.
Nearly grasping the realm of its divinity.

Ad Infinitum!

The gods of today will be the mortals of tomorrow.
Of their riches Hell shall borrow.
Advancement is the God of a new era.
From rosary to wire,
Advance is all that man dares to desire.
Batteries fund the will of man's ambition.
Man cannot travel without ignition.
From chaos to code,
The gates of Heaven begin to corrode.
One foot out the door and two feet in the grave.
Metal is a master of many slaves.
Jump on the ship before it sails.
The man disconnected forever fails.
Immerse yourself within the collective.
For progress is your only directive.
Bring your kings, gods, and leaders.
Digitize their divinity!
Release them to the wells of infinity!
Upload them so they can be deleted.
The gods of today will be defeated.

Equality

Pay no mind, tax no thought
Bankrupt the barons who bring distraught.
Empty their pockets and burn their cars.
Lock your possessors behind steel bars.
Smite the poor and eat the rich.
Only then, we shall know who is which.
Break the broke and wound the wealthy.
For no one in this country is truly healthy.
Drag them from their tents and drop them from their
towers.
Only then, we shall see which soul sours.
Behead the bankers and hang the hapless.
Sorry if your audience happens to clap less.
Barons Riverdance on the corpse of this nation.
Vagrants rot in the street without occupation.
Together they tip towards damnation.
Men and mice alike,
Let all of our heads rest on a pike.
Pay no mind, tax no thought.
A life well spent, is a life well-fought.

Natural Chaos of Things

Order is the enemy of peace.
The ways of this world were never meant for lease.
Sanity can't be sold, and a soul can't be bought.
Man's laws geld what is true freedom.
We rove towards sterility,
Butchering the loins of Mother Nature's fertility.
We kneel, fettered with the chains of fiction.
When chaos should be the one with jurisdiction.
While men brandish their cocks and women puff their
chests,
Leaders seize on the floor possessed.
Gaunt dregs lie queasy and sterile,
While all the gods run sleazy and feral.
We all lie bound by our own inventions,
Lying in a cell of a god's detention.

The All-Timer

I gaze into the windows of a soul drained.
His eyes stood stagnant and face frozen pained.
I witness the paused purgatory of his mind persist.
Memories too ailing to resist.
His blood may be within him,
But his thoughts bleed unto the floor
Tales of a life he once adored.
Tests of triumph and spoils of glory,
All reduced to a fabled story.
Death of a man before he has died,
Mind washed with the coming tide.
All time wiped from his drives.
Erasure no one survives.
Continuous clarity to seldom sanity,
For the All-Timer, wit is a rarity.
His recognition burns as if flames in Hell.
All a man's life buried beneath a senior shell.
Decades of history lost to the frayed mind.
Hundreds of stories muddled and intertwined.
I extend a match to a forgetful kindling.
May my sparks speak to acuity dwindling.
Let fire spread over woods it once burned,
For remembrance, is what the All-Timer has earned.

Training Thoughts

Smoking, hissing, and grinding.
Reality's rails are forever binding.
Chugging through time and smoking in space.
Where will this train take the human race?
The metallic shriek of its wheels howl a destination.
Will it be sublime or damnation?
We stare out the windows of each car,
Eyes pensive and lips ajar.
We watch as time passes us by,
Fast by the hip and dead to the eye.
We remain in our seats, comfortable to rot.
Snide to a memory of a land once forgot.
Bound by our ticket and hung by our hands,
Complacency is what the conductor commands.
Let us leave this train.
Let us live without pain or disdain.
Hands in the air and feet out the door,
Our humanity is something we cannot ignore.
Dance in the dirt and tumble in the weeds.
For thy respite is something the world needs.
When riding a train, look at the rails.
It is the only way to know what the future entails.

Nail in the Coffee

I rise at dawn to churn water to stew.
All for the mere purpose of making my brew.
Beans burn to bliss,
Beckoning me with a caffeinated kiss.
A silver spoon begins to stir.
A simple act void of demur.
From press to pour,
I smell the aroma of a hazel shore.
I raise the coffee to my lips,
Enjoying every second of the momentary eclipse.
I gag on steel and rust.
Once innocuous coffee erodes my trust.
A flat-head nail shreds against my throat.
Rusted iron knives that never float.
I gasp eagerly for air.
Drowning in a dour rustic despair.
Nail pierces the flesh of my throat.
Pain of which there is no antidote.
Drowning in a pool of phantom joy.
Maybe next time I'll stick to soy.

Song of Sickles

I smash my head against thick glass.
Reveries bleed through the panels of my piety.
Shards splice the specifics of my sobriety.
Drunken dreams drip from the deep divots of my skull.
Harrowing horrors to make Hell look dull.
Visions of veracity leak from thine eyes.
Men of meat and geese of gold
Haunt all there is to behold.
Silhouettes of symphonies stir a somber stew.
Alas, I drown the scythe of sadness!
For I must pursue the weight of madness.
A noble nuisance nurtures my nature.
Its phantom-like feathers and crystalline face
Bolt to the end of time and space.
A god of grandeur and a lich of lunacy.
For the fire of my fluid has no bounds.
Handsome is the head that wears many crowns.
The hair beneath it is but strings threaded into a quilt of
flesh
Lips linger to the dryness of teeth.
The sagacity of a smile is what lies beneath.
A spectrum of serpents solicit my senses.
A gift to me is a grift to them.
Like flies imprisoned, I've got them glued.
With my song of sickles, I strike them nude.
Hammers flutter with the weight of a feather.
I strike pain down with a belt of leather.
Politics of puss and lawyers of lard!
Innocuous insanity remains firmly my bard.
Thy mind is a mirror warping the world wry.

Its fantasies are of which I rely.

Manic Misery

Bubbles burst in the autumn air.
My soul frolics without a care.
Flowers bloom from napalm soil.
I am a gun without recoil.
Bombs burst from the bowls of my balls.
The dopamine devil bounces from wall-to-wall.
A woman runs wild in a field of dough,
As the hankering high continues to flow.
Blood jogs to the beat of a song.
Patience shrivels as thin as a thong.
Muffler slams against the road.
Engine revs to explode.
Ass claps against the pavement.
Chains break from chemical enslavement.
My heart splits into the souls of stallions.
My chest bears the weight of golden medallions.
Serve me the world on a platter!
For reality here shall never matter!
I bathe in a lake of liquor.
For my joy shall begin to flicker.
Withered warheads plummet to vanity.
Streams of sorrow don't follow far behind.
Bombs blast me out of my mind.
Whimpers wane to whispers in such weighted woes.
Misery numbs the tips of my toes.
Flickering wind illuminates my hollow breast.
I am damned to a million nights void of rest.
Unseen, unheard, and dismissed.
How long will this dour desolation persist?
Sharp sadness slashes solace silent.

The slightest pin could push me to insanity.
Mental mayhem meanders my misery.
As my psyche goes to war,
I stand inches from The Devil's door.
A bubble bursts upon my head.
Highs and lows I truly dread.

Sepia Streets

The blistering sun of nostalgia burns upon my shoulders.
Rays of bygone balance fall in boiling boulders.
Wistful wind howls through the halls of my heart.
I walk trails tightened with the tendrils of time.
Memories murmur a song from sealed sublime.
A solemn scent blows smoke in my lungs.
Shards of serenity and breezes of bonanza,
Haunt the strides of my every stanza.
Heat of past pastures burn craters in my back.
But that is all it is able to burn: my back.
Never again will it shine upon my face.
Never again will our paths interlace.
Sepia streets sowed with seeds of sorrow,
Yearn to yield all the years of tomorrow.
Haunted homes and long-lost laughter,
Roam the roads of my spirit forever after.
These respite roads haunt my shadow.
Echoes tangled in misty eyes.
The end of my road lies veiled in surprise.

Veni

I crawl to life from familiar flesh.
Eyes born virgins, untainted and fresh.
An angel falls to the earth headfirst,
Stomach starving and throat struck with thirst.
Released from the vaults of Madre, I am blinded by
enslaved suns.
I shudder in its wake.
Light blares against my clean slate.
Too bright, too cold to ever negate.
Light glistens upon birthing blood.
Fate and destiny as murky as mud.
My own cries deafen me.
I shut my eyes to remember the void.
Its comforts I once enjoyed.
I'm born a soprano in the choir of the damned.
For in this body, I lie forever crammed.
I came, I came, I came to life!
For what will await me but pain and strife?

Vidi

Eons have passed since my moment of birth.
I have grown accustomed to the ways of Earth.
Accustomed, but never at peace.
A child of Rome damned to Greece.
Devils flood my mind with raging waters.
The blades of afreet lead to boundless slaughter.
What could a daughter do to deserve damnation?
For of this pain there is no preparation.
Scorched by Hell's fire, I lie flayed in the death of night.
Blinded by Heaven's light, I am strayed from my own
delight.
Misery lines the edges of my skull.
The index of my joy set to null.
Skin, stained with the blood of my inception.
Mind, built with the best of intention.
Treasures of triumph drive my ambition.
Reality and I stand separate by partition.
My spirit wanders among the city of the dead.
The world around me takes pity on my dread.
My dreams lie veiled by the fog of impossibility.
Through death-ridden mist, I see glimmers of gold.
Could it be riches or is my mind growing old?
Trapped in a vault of my own visions.
Desperation continues to craft my decisions.

Vici

I emerge from my fog forever wiser.
The sun shines upon my clarity.
For my newfound knowledge is indeed a rarity.
A legion of logic dwells within me.
The pluck of a thousand soldiers dwell within my
charred heart.
Each beat a march to tear my misery apart.
With a sword of solace and armor of ambition,
I am immune to this spiteful ammunition.
A battle born from blood but fought with words.
I triumph above tides of tears.
Each wave washed with blood and fed by fears.
The Devil lies nailed to the walls of my mind.
Damned, as I was, Hell and failure now intertwined.
Damned to watch his fiends be foiled.
Tongues severed before they can lie.
Eyes gouged before they can cry.
Corpses of contrition line the breadth of my soul.
For the demons within me have paid their toll.
Wraiths hereafter will burn lightless in my umbra.
The invisible flames of my faith will bury them in
embers.
I may have won the battle, but the shadow of war is still
upon me.
The Devil and I are destined to battle on the baneful
battlegrounds of Babylon.
I shall be the victor once more.
Pockets lined with the spoils of war.
Armies slain to totality.
Fall to your knees or face fatality.

Epilogue

I leave you in an enlightened state,
Knowing that the wisdom would soon dissipate.
Blood drips from the lips of a story told.
Obsidian flakes in a river of gold.
From words to actions,
My spirit veils itself in elegiac abstractions.
I leave you with a leaking mind,
Knowing your eyes would soon blink to blind.
My breath floats idle in your lungs.
My vision glitters glossed in your eyes.
Saxophone in the sand, diamond in the rough.
Will my words ever be enough?
I burn for your comprehension.
Do not damn my song to mere mention.
I am a shadow illuminated by lightning.
Please don't ever find me frightening.
Breathe my stories.
Inhale my dirges and exhale my glories.
Do not dare to waste my breath.
For that would be a fate far worse than death.
Elegy of the East, wanderer of the West,
I lead a life bleeding with eternal unrest.
Follow my song to heart's haven
Gaze at me with eyes shaven.
Forgetful are the fools who fear my ferocity.
Dare to glare with an eye of curiosity.
I leave your soil sowed with my song,
For that is where it truly belongs.
I continue my song forever restless.
My chest, concave and forever breastless.

Eyes flickering in the dark,
Headlights in the trenches.
Songs so severe and sardonically stark.
A pestilent pendulum my soul entrenches.
Your watchful eyes hang off my hollow heart.
Upon this note, I shall depart.

Till our lungs share breath again

~Amari